Big Machines

by Annabelle Lynch

W
FRANKLIN WATTS
LONDON • SYDNEY

First published in 2013 by
Franklin Watts
338 Euston Road
London
NW1 3BH

Franklin Watts Australia
Level 17/207 Kent Street
Sydney
NSW 2000

Picture credits: Chukov/Shutterstock: 16-17.
Grant Glendinning/Shutterstock: cover, 14-15.
imagineegami/Shutterstock: 8-9. Gregory Johnston/
Shutterstock: 5. majeczka/Shutterstock: 6-7. My
Portfolio/Shutterstock: 18-19. Mihai Simonia/
Shutterstock: 12-13. smereka/Shutterstock: 10-11.
Jim Wileman/Alamy: 20-21.

Every attempt has been made to clear copyright.
Should there be any inadvertent omission please
apply to the publisher for rectification.

Franklin Watts is a division of Hachette Children's Books,
an Hachette UK company. www.hachette.co.uk

A CIP catalogue record for this book is
available from the British Library.

Dewey number: 629.2

ISBN 978 1 4451 1644 0 (hbk)
ISBN 978 1 4451 1650 1 (pbk)

Series Editor: Julia Bird
Picture Researcher: Diana Morris
Series Advisor: Catherine Glavina
Series Designer: Peter Scoulding

Printed in China

Contents

The words in **bold** can be found in the glossary.

Machines help us

Big machines help us do our work. They do all sorts of jobs on the road, on the building site and on the farm.

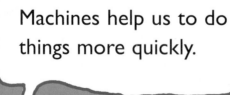

Machines help us to do things more quickly.

On the road

Lorries carry heavy loads from place to place. They can carry almost anything, from food and drink to clothes and toys.

This type of lorry is called a tanker.

Rubbish and recycling

Rubbish trucks pick up waste and take it to a tip. Some trucks take rubbish to be **recycled**.

The bin is emptied into the back of the truck.

Big
bulldozers

Bulldozers move earth, rocks and **rubble**. They scoop them up or push them along with a **blade**.

Bulldozers work on building sites.

Digging diggers

Diggers are tough machines that dig holes and **trenches**. They can go over rocky ground and through thick mud.

Diggers come in all shapes and sizes.

Super Cranes

Cranes move, lift and lower heavy loads on the building site. They reach up high into the sky!

This crane is helping to build a block of flats.

Tough tractors

Tractors are used to do all sorts of jobs on a farm. They carry and pull things across muddy fields.

This tractor is pulling a **plough**.

Helpful
harvesters

Big machines called combine harvesters are used to cut down and **gather** crops on the farm.

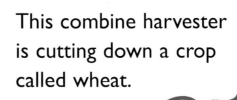

This combine harvester is cutting down a crop called wheat.

 Go and see!

There are farms and **theme parks** where you can try some big machines for yourself. Have fun!

This boy is trying out a digger.

Glossary

blade - a metal plate with a sharp edge

gather - put together

plough - a machine that is pulled across a field to turn the soil over

recycle - to break down something so that the things it is made from can be used again

rubble - big bits of broken stone and brick

theme park - a place where you can go on rides and try out different games and machines

trench - a long ditch in the ground

Websites:

http://kids.discovery.com/tell-me/machines/big-construction-machines

http://www.diggerland.com

Every effort has been made by the Publishers to ensure that the websites are suitable for children, and that they contain no inappropriate or offensive material. However, because of the nature of the Internet, it is impossible to guarantee that the contents of these sites will not be altered. We strongly advise that Internet access is supervised by a responsible adult.

Quiz

Use the information in the book to answer these questions.

1. Name three places where you can find big machines.

2. What do bulldozers move?

3. What do we use cranes to do?

4. Which machine is used to cut down and gather crops on the farm?

5. Where could you try using a big machine for yourself?

The answers are on page 24.

Answers

1. On the road, on a building site and on a farm
2. Earth, rocks and rubble
3. To move, lift and lower heavy loads
4. A combine harvester
5. At a farm or theme park

Index